Angels of Burma

For Alan –
with best wishes, I hope
you enjoy the Book.
from The Author
Diane

Angels of Burma

Diane Sloggett
(later Mackenzie)

The Pentland Press
Edinburgh – Cambridge – Durham – USA

© Diane Sloggett, 2000

First published in 2000 by
The Pentland Press Ltd
1 Hutton Close
South Church
Bishop Auckland
Durham

ISBN 1-85821-788-1

Typeset by Carnegie Publishing, Carnegie House, Chatsworth Road, Lancaster
Printed and bound by Bookcraft (Bath) Ltd

*To my son, Mark, in remembrance
of your Mother's war work*

Contents

Foreword

A Short History of the VAD Unit, India, 1944 to 1946

IN 1944 LADY LOUIS MOUNTBATTEN recruited 200 Red Cross and St John's Ambulance to go out to the Front Line Hospitals in Burma to help the over-worked Military Nurses attached to the 14th Army. Many of them ill-trained, they were pushed to their utmost under poor living conditionds and in intense heat learning how to deal with severe burns cases, give morphia and administer the new wonder drug, penicillin.

This is the story of one of them, an untrained 19 year old, described in moving detail.

It starts with their departure in the middle of the night under extreme secrecy from a deserted Euston Station via a roundabout route to Greenock, embarking on the *Strathnaver* packed to overflowing with troops, in convoy protected by a fleet of destroyers, to the Suez Canal where the blackout was lifted and they saw lights for the first time in four years.

On arrival in Bombay they were taken to Poona by ambulance train to become acclimatised and they served briefly in the local hospital there. When their postings came through they were split up into groups of 10 and 12. It meant little to them, just the number of a Field Hospital in SEAC. The journey via Calcutta to Panitola Hospital took several days and nights of continuous travelling in unlit and overheated trains.

On arrival they were sent on to the Indian and British wards, ignorant of the caste customs and unable to speak Urdu.

The book tells of life in the hospital, the friendships, the hard work, the fun when off-duty and at Christmas time, night duty alive with hazards and strange noises when jackals prowled, the night a goat wandered into one of the open-hutted wards and lay on a bed. It also tells of the writer's whirlwind romance, of being whisked off to Calcutta to get married to a Chindit Officer she had only known for a week.

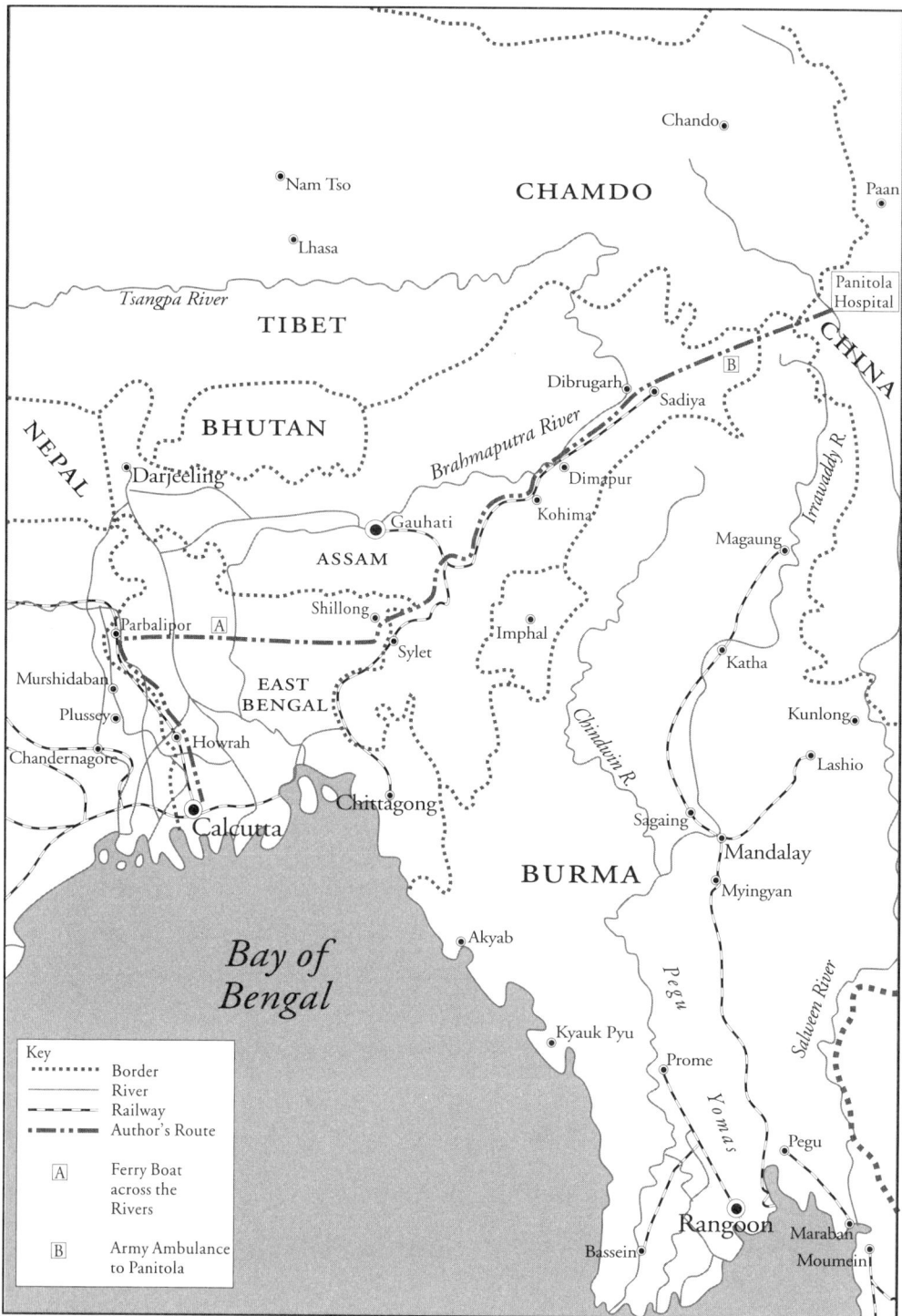

Key

·········	Border
———	River
— — —	Railway
—··—··—	Author's Route
[A]	Ferry Boat across the Rivers
[B]	Army Ambulance to Panitola

Nam Tso

Lhasa

Chando

Paan

CHAMDO

Panitola Hospital

Tsangpa River

TIBET

CHINA

BHUTAN

Darjeeling

Dibrugarh

Sadiya

[B]

Brahmaputra River

Dimapur

NEPAL

Gauhati

Kohima

ASSAM

Magaung

Irrawaddy R.

Shillong

Parbalipor

[A]

Sylet

Imphal

Murshidaban

Katha

Plussey

EAST BENGAL

Chindwin R.

Kunlong

Chandernagore

Howrah

Lashio

Chittagong

Calcutta

Sagaing

Mandalay

BURMA

Myingyan

Akyab

Pegu

Salween River

Bay of Bengal

Kyauk Pyu

Prome

Yomas

Pegu

Rangoon

Maraban

Bassein

Moumeini

Chapter One

I WAS WORKING as an ordinary SJAB Nurse in a convalescent Home called Lake House Hospital in Wiltshire on the edge of Salisbury Plain. The house was the beautiful home of Lady Janet Bailey. One day in early June 1944 our County Superintendent rang me up and said, 'Would you like to volunteer for India?' I had told her on several occasions that I would like to serve overseas, and that was the start of a great adventure that I shall never forget all my life.

Soon after my name was sent in I was told to report to HQ in Belgrave Square for a selection Board – which was a great ordeal! When I arrived there were some twenty others waiting, and as time passed more arrived. We had to go in singly to the interview room and afterwards were let out by a different door, so there was no opportunity of asking a previous interviewee what questions had been asked. However the buzz went round that there was a catch question asking if one minded nursing Indian troops as opposed to the British Tommies. It was vital to answer that of course one did not mind. The Board consisted of the Countess Mountbatten, Dame Beryl Oliver who was the Head of the Red Cross and several senior Officers of the RAMC, Red Cross and St John. They sat in a semi-circle and the one to be interviewed was seated alone in front of them at a small table. A daunting prospect for a young 18 year old.

It was considered very important that the girls sent should represent the highest aims and ideals of the two orders, for each one was to be in a way an Ambassador to that faraway country. If you passed your selection Board you were sent down to the department MI of the War Office for a medical examination – so one knew soon enough the result of one's interview.

Then followed a feverish few weeks of equipping oneself with tropical uniform and getting one's kit in order, inoculations, vaccinations etc. I remember so well the small piece of equipment which impressed me more than all the rest – a white armband with a large red cross on it – which I was told would have to be worn if one was rescuing wounded under fire. This inspired me with great philanthropy, although I might add I never had occasion to wear it.

At the end of June, just about the time when the big offensive was in full swing in Burma and the tide of war was at last being turned in our favour, I received instructions to report to an address in London. We had by now been enrolled as VAD members of the order and been issued with little enamel roses to wear on our left lapel as an emblem of the Burma Unit. This first detachment to be sent out numbered about 200, so we were spread amongst various hostels in London for assembling. I went to a Salvation Army Guest House in Baker Street. The first girl I spoke to on arriving and who helped me with my luggage became my dearest friend, we remained together all the time, and I am now in fact godmother to her eldest child.

Immediately on arrival we were told that our movements were to be cloaked in the greatest secrecy and we might remain in London a night or two or a week or two. This was somewhat of an anti-climax, for I had fondly envisaged us sailing that very evening. We did in fact remain exactly a week, during which time Lady Louis Mountbatten, as she was then, invited the St John's members to her private house for tea, chatted to us all individually asking us to be sure and write her how we were getting on. I did in fact write to her after I had been out there some while, and received a very nice personal letter in reply.

We were allowed to telephone our parents, but as we did not

6

know ourselves when we were leaving this presented no problem. I remember a boyfriend came up to London to see me from the Convalescent Home near Salisbury and he took me out for the evening. He was a Glider Pilot, later to serve in the Arnheim Raid. He was very fond of me and we stayed out very late. I was anxious to get back to the hostel as I was terrified that I would return to find everyone had left without me.

Finally we left in the dead of night, piled into the backs of open trucks and the chance passers-by in the streets all waved to us for they guessed we were bound for some theatre of operations. We had no idea what port we were leaving from, we arrived at a deserted Kings Cross Station and were ushered into the third class compartment of the only train there. The journey was interminable, for thirty hours we travelled by every roundabout route until we finally arrived at Greenock. We saw the enormous convoy of ships that we were joining, which explained why all the secrecy had been so necessary. We were taken out to the SS *Strathnaver* which was packed to overflowing with troops, all leaning over the ship's rail, letting out cheers and wolf-whistles when they perceived that the tender full of girls was coming alongside.

Chapter Two

THE CABIN THAT I FOUND MYSELF IN was enormous, with rows and rows of double bunks lined up very close to each other. Marion, my friend, whom I had met on that first day arriving at the hostel, and I had remained close together throughout the journey, and we pounced on a bunk near the doorway. I took the upper and she the lower bunk. Our suitcases went underneath. Next day, our first day aboard, after a very good breakfast, a treat after years of wartime rationing, we were all given our special envelopes and wrote out letters. There was not a great deal of time as they had to be handed in by 11.30. During the afternoon we had boat-drill, which being the first was of course, a complete shambles and all the VADs made complete fools of themselves. After dinner, a marvellous meal, with as much butter and sugar as we wanted, we weighed anchor. Everyone went on deck to watch. As I stood there watching the mountains of Scotland receding into the distance, I had the most complete feeling of being alone. Now there was no turning back. I was leaving everyone I loved and everything I had ever known and setting off for who knew how many years. It all seemed rather like a dream as the other ships fell into place before and behind and we steamed out of the Clyde. I was terribly moved and stood among hundreds of other people thronging the rails – yet completely alone.

When I awoke next morning I looked out of the porthole and saw miles of open sea. The convoy had grown during the night, there were ships all round and away in the distance our guardian destroyers. I went up on deck before breakfast and experienced very much the same feeling as the night before. I knew it was true but found it hard to believe that I was travelling in a troop ship, in convoy right out in the Atlantic. From now on we wore our life jackets and clip on lights all the time. The sea was a bit choppy but nothing to worry about. The ship was so large one did not notice the swell. I got a bit bored and depressed during late afternoon and evening. The inactivity of sitting around all day or pacing the deck was getting me down.

July 20th. The sea was becoming bluer, and by the afternoon it was quite hot. The deck looked rather like Margate or Blackpool on a Bank Holiday. My friend Marion and I had tied up with a few other girls and we had our own little select party on a particular corner of the deck. Some of the girls had formed attachments with some of the officers and romances were springing up. That evening there was a sing-song. I pushed my way through the crowd to the rails, where one could see the lower deck and looked down. There I saw something I shall not forget ... hundreds and hundreds of men, so closely packed that it looked like a patchwork quilt of khaki, Air Force Blue and Navy Blue. They were all singing at the tops of their voices – 'It's a long way to Tipperary', the words floating out over the sea, men who were on their way to fight somewhere, not knowing when, or if, they would ever come back. I suddenly felt terribly out of place amongst them, a woman somehow did not fit into this picture.

July 31st. We have passed Gibraltar and Malta and have seen Algiers and Tunis from a distance. We have been hugging the North African Coast for several days now. Looking through binoculars one can see the long stretches of arid sandy wastes with little white villages clustering together. That morning I was awakened early with the sound of depth charges being dropped from our accompanying destroyers. I don't remember being particularly frightened, at that age nothing seems to scare one and there is only the briefest entry of this in the diary that I kept on board. Our convoy had shrunk by now, some ships had left us after Gib. when we reached the Mediterranean presumably for an invasion of the South of France.

August 1st. Port Said today – the gateway to the East. We could see everything very clearly, the brightly coloured houses with verandas running all round, the mosques and domes and the Egyptian and British soldiers walking along the water's edge. We were the first big convoy to go through the Suez Canal. Each ship entered in single file, and as there was no stopping on the Mediterranean side, each ship passed in as soon as possible, one behind the other. It was much narrower than I had thought, we seemed very close to the bank on either side. Little groups of natives were squatting on their haunches on the banks of the Canal, some completely nude and diving into the water. They all waved at us. For some miles we passed bleak sandy wastes interspersed with Army tents. There were coloured and white soldiers walking about in the heat of the midday sun, then the scenery changed, little villages, palm trees fountains, white building and grass.

That evening we anchored in Suez harbour, with all the lights twinkling. That was the first time in five years that there had been a night for me without a 'blackout'. We could hardly believe our eyes for until then the ship had been plunged into darkness so as not to give our position away. One of the girls in our little group had a birthday party, and we all sat out on the deck drinking, smoking and looking at the lights of Suez. I found it hard to believe that this was not all a dream – that these girls sitting round me, whom 3 weeks ago I had never met, were not just part of that dream – yet at the same time I knew it to be true and home was many thousands of miles away.

August 2nd. Anchored at Port Tufique. All day boats had kept coming alongside, loading us up with fuel and provisions. I spent hours leaning out of my porthole or over the side of the deck watching the Egyptians in the barges below. They all looked to me terribly poor and ragged, and scrambled and fought for the coins, cigarettes and even sweets or crumbs of biscuits that the troops threw over to them. It was getting very hot now and everyone was starting to sweat and avoid the sun. The awnings were up over the deck to give shade, but we consoled ourselves by saying the worst was yet to come.

Chapter Three

I AM UNABLE TO WRITE about the last lap of our voyage across the Indian Ocean as for some reason I stopped writing my diary at that time. I seem to remember I got involved in a romance with a young RAF Officer on board, which might have accounted for it! Fortunately I found some notes which I made at a later date, once we had arrived in India, which have been a great help, for memories dim after a gap of fifty years although some of the experiences are still very vivid in my mind.

On the 15th August we finally docked at Bombay, and an ambulance train took us to a place called Kirkee, which is just outside Poona. Here we were to remain for a week or two in a transit camp to become accustomed to the way of life, the climate, the people and the food. The transit camp was in an empty wing of the hospital at Kirkee and whilst we were there we would do elementary duties on the wards. It was a joy to have fresh water and to be able to get really clean again after so long at sea. In no time the buzz went round that 200 young girls had just arrived out from England, and the invitations poured in. War weary officers who had not seen a woman for months and who were on leave in Poona after fighting in the jungle under dreadful conditions queued up to take us out every evening and we had a lovely time. The Governor's wife gave a ball for us at Government House and we all wore our clean caps aprons and dresses. During the course of the evening a tall young man wearing the badges of General Wingate's highly trained jungle fighters, the Chindits, came over and asked me to dance. It was an old fashioned waltz and we whirled round and round the room at great speed, to the music of the Blue Danube. Later he came and asked me to dance again and invited me to go with him to the races the following day. I had to refuse as I was already going with someone else. The following evening I was having dinner at the Poona Club with my date when I saw this young man come in surrounded by friends, apparently he had had a very good win at the races that afternoon and they were all in very good form. As I looked across I was sorry that I was not with them, and regretted having refused him the night before.

A few days later when I was on duty one morning at the Kirkee Hospital the Chindit Officer turned up on my ward. He was visiting some of his men who had been wounded during the recent fighting, so we had the chance to have a little talk and this time I was able to accept his invitation to got to the races with him the following weekend.

During this period we were given our cholera and plague injections, and issued with our camp kit, which consisted of a folding frame with a canvas bag slung on it. This was the wash basin! The canvas bath was very much on the same lines, but much lower down and the canvas bag somewhat larger! One had to sit cross-legged in this and being tall, I found this a most uncomfortable operation. We were also issued with a folding camp bed, a bucket and a camp chair. All this packed up fairly compactly and was to be the only personal furniture we would have for our use for a long time.

A cutting from a leading Bombay newspaper stated: 'Newly arrived from Britain are more than 200 members of Voluntary Aid Detachments of the Red Cross and St John organisations. The first VADs to assist military nurses overseas in this way, they will soon play an important part in the nursing and rehabilitation of men of the 14th Army, who have been wounded in the Burma fighting. They have been brought out to India to assist in the overworked military nursing services, whose establishment, especially on the Indian side, is greatly below strength. They gained considerable experience among injured in British Emergency Hospitals when the German blitzes were at their height.'

We also received much publicity in other newspapers and press shots were taken of us. We were given lectures on security and on the importance of complete secrecy in regard to anything we might hear about troop movements, that our letters home would be censored, therefore we had to be very careful what we wrote, not giving any indication of where we were to our parents, except that we were going to forward hospitals on the Burma Front. This latter was not so difficult for us as we were not allowed to see any maps and when we were eventually posted to our respective units, none of us had the faintest idea where we were. All I knew was that we were somewhere in Northern Assam on account of the Tea Plantations.

Finally our posting came through and the exciting moment arrived when we were told where we were to be sent. For most of us it meant little, just the number of a field or hutted hospital somewhere in SEAC. Each one of us had been allowed to choose a particular friend to be with as a companion, someone we could relax with when off duty. Marion and I chose to be together just as we had been on board ship. We were to be split up into groups of 8, 10, or 14, according to the size of the hospital. Marion and I had been posted with 8 others to an Indian British Hospital at a place called Panitola.

That afternoon we were allowed out to do any last minute shopping, and when I got back to the transit camp some hours later, the Senior Ward sister came to find me saying that there was a young man outside who had been patiently waiting for me for the last couple of hours. She said that I could go out and see him but that I was not allowed to leave the hospital grounds. It was of course

Alastair, the Chindit Officer whom I had become friendly with. He told me that he had come to let me know that orders had come through that his unit were to return on active service early the next morning, that he had come to say goodbye, but unfortunately as he had been waiting for quite a while he would not be able to stay long. We walked around the grounds of the transit camp holding hands and talking. I told him that we also were on the move and I was able to give him my new Army Post Office address. We talked of all sorts of things, our homes, families, the future, anything but the war against the Japanese. We both promised to write and then he was gone.

The following day we left, packed into a train for Calcutta, a journey of three days and nights of continuous travelling with the blinds of the carriage drawn both day and night. There were only stops for refuelling the engine, and we were not allowed out of the train. Looking back, one wonders how one managed to survive such conditions. Life today has become so easy and comfortable, but we had all been used to five years of wartime England, most important of all we were all fired by the enthusiasm of youth and embarking on a great adventure into the unknown. Hot meals were served by the ward boys, mainly curries, and the hygiene was primitive to say the least. We passed the time resting, sleeping, playing cards and trying to read in the dim light.

Finally on arriving at Calcutta a very different sight met our eyes from the comparative quiet and cleanliness of Poona. Little Indian children dressed literally in rags crowded up to the train as we alighted, all pushing and shoving each other, begging for coins and cigarettes and the platform was crowded with natives squatting on their hind legs. We were met by an Army Transport Officer, who organised a fleet of coolies to carry our baggage. I saw two little coolies, both of them half my height, one of them with my enormous heavy tin trunk balanced on his head, the same trunk that my father and the gardener could hardly carry between them when I had left home so many moons ago, the other one with my bulky camp kit on his head and my suitcase balanced precariously on top of it. We were led to some waiting lorries and the coolies loaded our luggage on to some trucks alongside. We were then whisked off at great speed through teeming streets to the centre of town. Everything around us seemed to be so dirty and smelly and everywhere thousands of people crowded the pavements. Finally we reached the Grand Hotel in Chowringee facing a large public park. The Grand was the best hotel in Calcutta and frequented by most of the officers who were in the city on leave. The main hall was crowded with them, and our arrival caused enormous interest, many trying to make dates with us before we had even had time to book in.

I had decided to telephone Bob Adam, the RAF Officer whom I had an affair with on the ship. He had told me that he was to join his squadron in Calcutta, and if I was ever there to be sure and ring him up at his Mess. As luck would have it he was there and of course delighted to hear from me, and said he would come down that evening and take me out. He brought a friend with him for my friend Marion and we went to the Saturday Club which was the smartest place in town and had a wonderful evening.

Our stopover in Calcutta, however, was not destined to be prolonged. We were urgently needed at the front and we had come out to nurse the soldiers of the 'Forgotten Army', so we were all pleased to be on our way when we received our marching orders 48 hours later.

Chapter Four

Now came the parting of the ways, and we split up into our various little groups. Our party consisted of nine of us under the supervision of Marion Robertson. All our luggage was carried out of the Grand Hotel and loaded into a waiting lorry. The heat was intense, and all the porters were shouting at once. We piled into a separate lorry and headed for the railway station, speeding through the crowded streets, the rickshaws and other traffic all hooting their horns and going as fast as us. We were to travel on the Assam Mail. This meant little to us as we still had no idea where Panitola was. We knew that it would be a long journey and that we would have to crossed the Bramaputra in a ferry to reach the forward area which was under the control of the army.

We finally reached the station. The Assam Mail was due to leave in 15 minutes and in that time we had to unload all our luggage which amounted to 40 pieces, there were 10 of us and each one had a tin trunk, one suitcase, a bedding roll and a big canvas bag of camp equipment, all this to get through the chaos of the station. There were no seats reserved for us as the RTO had never heard of VADs and we had been booked on a troop train thinking we were men. However a kindly sergeant found one empty carriage at the back of the train, our luggage was piled in after us, the whistle blew and we were off.

We were in a Third Class carriage with a wooden bench running down each side and a little smelly lavatory at one end. We had been told to take sandwiches and fill our water bottles so at least we had something. We nibbled at our food and drank from our bottles, as our small carriage got hotter and hotter and the smell worse and worse as we jogged through the Bengal countryside. The train seemed to stop at every single station. We had to change trains that evening at the junction for Darjeeling, at a place called Parbatipur (see map). We arrived there at about 10 p.m., dreading the thought of all the hassle that would ensue with all our baggage and clamouring porters but we were in for a nice surprise. There was an English RTO with two Sergeants carrying hot mugs of tea. 'We had a signal from Calcutta about you,' he said, 'and about the unsavoury accommodation you had to endure for all these hours so we have reserved a first class carriage for you with comfortable bunks and good clean WCs.' We were told we could sleep till morning, when we would change again to cross the Brahmaputra. We asked them if they had heard of Panitola, they said they had, but were a bit vague about when we would arrive.

Next morning we dressed ready for the next change. Marion Robertson stayed behind with another VAD called Jean, to help with the luggage while the rest of us went on ahead to the ferry boat. On arrival we settled down with a group of Army Officers who had been on the same train and enjoyed a very nice breakfast. A press photographer appeared and took our photos for the SEAC newspaper, the caption was to be: 'VADs over the Bramaputra'.

Crossing in the ferry took quite a long time as the river is very wide. On arrival at the other side we were met by a major from the hospital at Gauhati. He was very kind and helpful, taking us to our new train and dealing with the luggage and clamouring porters. We were now in the forward area where the railway had been taken over by the Army. For some reason our first class carriage which we had been allocated had been stripped, no seat paddings, no electric light bulbs or water in the lavatories, but at least we had our luggage and nothing had been lost. We had another 20 hours to travel in this train. The kindly Major had asked the Army Officers, we had chummed up with on the boat to look after us, as they were going on the same train. They invited us to meet them in the Buffet Car for lunch and we accepted willingly. We stayed there most of the day. We talked all the time and they were very interested to hear all about our adventures since we had arrived in India. They paid for all our meals and the time passed very pleasantly. When the time came to go back to our compartment there were affectionate goodbyes and in some cases addresses were exchanged. They had to get out at Dimapur in the middle of the night and travel by road to Imphal (see map) to be ready for the big push against the Japs which was to come. When we got back to our compartment we laid out our bed-rolls by the light of our torches and fell into an exhausted sleep.

Next morning at our final stop we were met by two ambulances, one for our luggage and one for us, as the last part of the journey was to be done by road. We were now in Northern Assam. The road we bumped along was a straight dirt road full of pot-holes and it seemed to go on for ever surrounded on each side by tea plantations. Finally we arrived at the hospital.

My first view of the hospital was a low long hut with a straw roof which was the Out-Patients or Reception ward. All the wards were like this, most of them joined by a raised covered way. Our quarters were on the other side of the road, the entrance guarded by two Sepoy soldiers. A very nice sister greeted us and said that she would show us around and help us to settle in. Her name was Sister Bapti.

Our quarters were certainly primitive but at least we were not in tents and we did not need our camp beds. We were allocated in twos to a small hut which was called a basha. It had a straw thatched roof, and there were five of them in a row joined by a raised walkway. These were to be the VAD's quarters. We paired off as usual, each one of us with our friend. Marion and I took the second hut, and the others sorted themselves out as they wished. The basha was

View of the hospital

furnished with two wooden beds, the base being plaited ropes instead of springs, these were known as charpois, and were, although one might not have thought so, surprisingly comfortable. Mosquito nets hung from wires overhead to be tucked in under the mattress.

A locally made chest of drawers and a hanging cupboard to be shared between us was all the rest of the furniture. Beyond was an annex room for our camp bath, basin and canvas pail to be placed. The concrete floor was sloping so that the water would run away, and there in the corner was the lavatory, known by all as a 'thunderbox'. This was in fact a wooden seat with a bucket inside. Sister explained to us the complex system of caste, which we knew nothing about. The thunderbox would be emptied by the sweeper, no one else would do this job, also our baths would be filled by the water carrier and no one else, and our room would be cleaned and laundry taken away by the bearer. We had to be very careful, she said, to stick by this as it was part of their Hindu religion. I remember years later when I was living in Army quarters in Hong Kong, asking the cookboy to water the flowers on the verandah, and he gave me his notice as it was an insult to his caste to ask him to carry water.

The QAs, i.e. the trained nursing sisters were similarly housed and we shared their mess and fed with them. Our first evening we went through to the mess for supper dressed in woollen slacks that were far too hot and white cotton shirts that we had been issued with before leaving, the same that we had worn on board ship. Matron nearly had a fit when she saw us. What had they been thinking of back in Poona to send us to the jungle in such clothes? What about malaria precautions? The people in the hospitals in Poona had no idea of conditions with the 14th Army, it was like another world. Possibly part of the reason for this was the rigid security as far as 'talk' was concerned, and all men returning from the fighting areas had been instructed not to discuss the appalling conditions or the movements of troops in any way. Down in Poona they were hardly aware there was a war going on. I remember one evening during the period that we were down there being asked out to dinner by a fairly senior officer, and he took me to the elegant restaurant at the Turf Club. After some discussion a small table was laid for us in the corridor outside. My escort explained it was because I was not wearing a long dress. I remember being furious. Before leaving home I had packed one nice dress to wear for 'occasions', it was in pale grey with a pretty white floral design and small buttons down the front, to be worn in fact at a later date, as my wedding dress. My escort was on the Staff in Poona and used to the life

Marion and myself at the entrance to the hospital

of smart society entertaining which was still going on in spite of there being a war on. He was apologetic but not as angry as I was. We had come from an England at war for five years and all the deprivations that went with it, and I was on my way to join another war, against the Japanese this time, and I was not considered good enough to dine in the restaurant because I was not in evening dress and put to feed in the corridor!

The Matron of our hospital, known as 49 IBGH which stood for Indian British General Hospital, was a warm understanding woman, we were lucky. I think she was Irish, she was fairly stout I remember and had reddish hair. She realised that we had all been thrown in at the deep end, that we were not used to the climate, did not speak a word of Urdu and that we had arrived ill prepared with the most unsuitable clothes. (Many of these problems were ironed out later for the units of VADs who were sent out from England to follow us as a result of complaints made by our Commandant Miss Corsair to the Chief Matron in Delhi.) she gave us all the day off on the morning following our arrival to go into the Bazaar to get suitable clothes. We set off in an Army Lorry to the 'shops'. There was an Officers' Shop at a place some distance away, where we could buy khaki material. The House Sister who had met us on our arrival, came with us to advise on what we should need, and how much to buy. Marion and I decided to get some extra khaki drill of a better quality, to have a smart bush jacket made for off duty wear in the evenings. We then returned to the village of Panitola, which consisted of a long line of ramshackle huts, stretching for about half a mile on both sides of the main road. There were bars and eating places, men selling drinks, fruit, local food and all the usual commodities that one sees in bazaars all over India. Sitting crossed legged in front of a hut with a large sign in English which said 'Military Tailor' sat an old man with a long white beard. He soon collected some of his friends and relations to measure us all up and promised us that we should each have one shirt and one pair of slacks by 5 p.m. that evening. The rest of our orders would follow in a few days time. To us this seemed like a miracle, but with hindsight one knows that a traveller on a cruise ship calling in to Singapore or Hong Kong in the morning can order a beautifully tailored suit in the morning to be delivered on board ship in time to set sail that evening.

We also bought ourselves a hurricane lamp each, to be able to see our way around in the evenings. This came in very useful later on, when we went on night duty. By day we would be wearing our ordinary nurses' uniform with starched caps, but without aprons.

Next morning at 8 a.m. we went on duty. I was assigned to a BOR Surgical Ward. (British Other Ranks). My sister-in-charge was called Sister Francis, she was small and pretty and very nice. One of us had been sent to each ward and one to do duty in the operating theatre. Some of us had more experience than others, having worked at home in Military or Naval Hospitals after Dunkirk and during

Scottie, my RAMC orderly who me helped so much

the Blitz. I think I probably had the least experience of all of them for as stated at the beginning of this story I was working in a Convalescent Home in Wiltshire as a St John's Ambulance Nurse when I was recruited as a VAD. My duties there had been mainly to make beds, take temperatures, carry trays of food from the kitchen and help with the washing up. All the patients in the Convalescent Home were walking wounded and were able to do all their personal things for themselves. However, wisely I had kept very quiet about this, even to my best friend. Fortunately for me that first week was fairly slack and the hospital was half empty, but they had been overflowing before with Chindit casualties being flown out from North Burma.

The staff on my ward consisted of Sister, two RAMC Orderlies and myself. One of the orderlies was called Scottie. I remember his name because I have several photographs of him in my album. Scottie was an absolute godsend. He helped me so much, realising how green I was, and under his tuition during those first few days, I was able to conceal from Sister Francis my lack of hospital experience.

The ward was a long low wooden hut, with a thatched roof, flanked on either side with a kind of covered verandah, there were beds everywhere, inside and out, these same charpois that I have already described, covered with red army blankets. At the foot of each charpoi hung a card with the patient's name, number, and unit. The week that I arrived many of the beds were empty, but these conditions were not to last long. At one end of the ward was the treatments room and at the other the ablutions. As there was only one Nursing Sister and two orderlies to a ward one could see how short-staffed they were. It meant that with the arrival of the VADs the overworked QAs were able to get some off-duty, leaving one of us in charge instead of just an orderly. We were not expected to empty the bedpans, this was done by the medical orderlies as we were not allowed to enter the latrines. The VADs who were sent to work on the Indian wards had to get used to the caste system. They could not ask their nursing sepoy to empty the bedpan, this had to be done by the sweeper. He would not be allowed to touch the food, this was prepared by the wardboy. The nurses were not allowed to touch the food either, and it was very difficult for them to give medicine, as they must not touch the patients' mouths with the glass. The patient just opened his mouth and the medicine was poured straight down. I did not have these problems at first, but some months later when the hospital moved to Dibrugah I was put in charge of an Indian VD ward. I felt very important having such a responsibility, and when I wrote home to my parents about it, I received a very irate letter back from my father saying that he thought it was an absolute disgrace that a young girl of my age should have been assigned to a VD ward. Of course at home they really had no idea of what it was like out there and we had to be so guarded about what we wrote.

The walking patients who were now recovering and waiting to be sent back to the base hospitals, from whence they would be posted back to their units, were a great help. It was satisfying for them to be able to help their mates and it gave them something to do to relieve the boredom. There was one soldier on my ward who was a great help. His name was Winchester, and I am sure he was kept on longer than necessary because he made himself so useful. He used to help me make the beds, help turn the patients over, fetch bedpans and bottles and remove them.

A lot of duties which are not normally done by untrained staff in hospitals at home, had to be done by us through force of circumstance – there was no one else to do it! Things like the giving of morphia injections and other drugs, 'prepping' the patient for the operating theatre, dressing abdominal wounds where there were sometimes tubes draining off the blood, and other delicate dressings. However one learnt quickly through experience. I remember well the

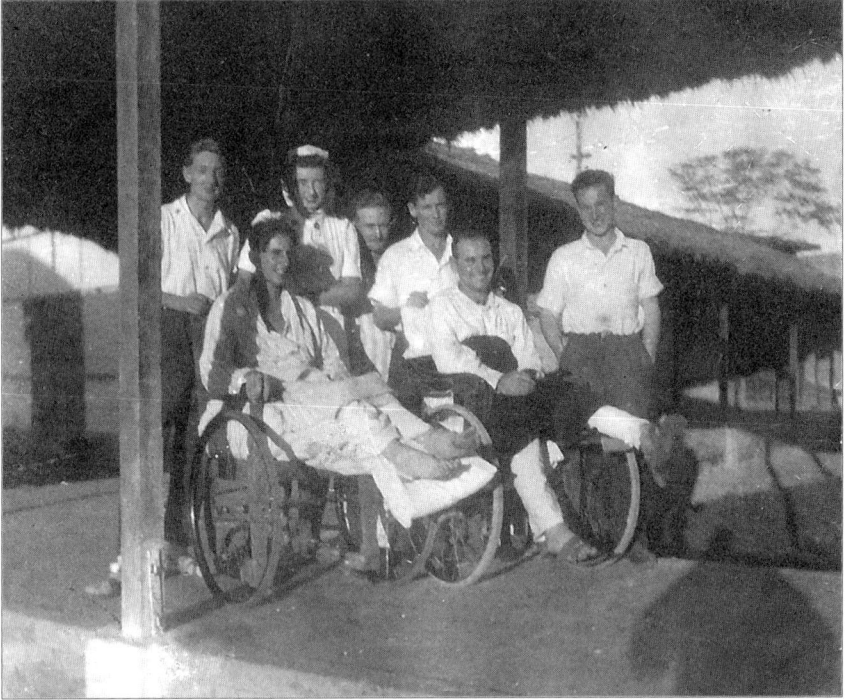

Myself and Winchester wheeling the boys down to watch football

first time I was told to give a morphia injection. I had never given one before, and it wasn't so much the fear of hitting a vein, or of injecting air as well as the drug into the patient which would have been very painful, as the idea of thrusting this large needle into him. I hesitated and hesitated and just could not bring myself to do it. Sister Francis was very understanding about this, and in spite of being very busy, did it for me, and said, 'We will choose the opportunity when we have a patient who is in great pain for you to give your first injection, then if you do it badly and hurt him, it will be nothing compared to the other pain he is suffering and he won't even notice it!' Which is certainly the method of learning by trial and error! However it worked, as shortly afterwards a patient returned from the operating theatre having had his left leg amputated as far as the thigh – he was suffering greatly after he came round from the anaesthetic for he complained of agonizing pains in the leg that was no longer there. Sister called me. 'Nurse, now is your opportunity,' she said, 'give the poor boy some morphia.' He was under far too great a stress to notice my nervousness or my amateur approach and I plunged the needle in, and did it all right. That was the first of many hundreds of injections of different drugs, and as one gained confidence, so one gained skill. Then there was the administering of the new wonder drug penicillin, which had only recently been discovered and saved so many lives during the last war. The man responsible for this great invention Alexander Fleming is buried in the crypt of St Paul's Cathedral, his cremated remains are honoured behind a plaque in the shrine of the Order of the British Empire.

Most VADs had had little or no experience of penicillin before. The precious liquid had to be kept in a refrigerator. We learnt how to prepare it and also how to administer it, by injecting the needle deep into the muscle. Another new experience for most of us was gangrene, for at home this is not so common, whereas in the tropics infections sets in so quickly when men have been lying in damp fly infected undergrowth maybe for many hours before receiving medical attention. The smell of a gangrenous wound is appalling, until you get used to it, sufficient to make one feel really ill, and the affected area is all black and very unpleasant to look upon. One day I was working on the ward by myself as Sister was off duty, when a young soldier was brought in who had been very badly shot in the backside. Gangrene had set in and his buttocks were practically eaten away, the flesh was black and the smell terrible. I never thought he would live. He had to lie on his face for days, but with regular penicillin injections and careful dressings morning and evening he got better. It was my duty to do his dressings, it took ages removing the old ones, and replacing with wet saline gauze all over the lower part of his body. Scottie helped me with this job, and the three of us would chatter away trying to cheer him up, and after some while when he started to improve the satisfaction on my part was enormous, as I felt that he was my particular patient. When he was well enough to walk, he was flown out to the base hospital and I was really sad to see him go.

Earlier on I mentioned that the slack period was not to last long, for soon after heavy fighting broke out round a place called Pen-wei. The wounded were flown straight out to the little make-shift airstrip which served our hospital, having had their First Aid at the forward Dressing Station. The only possible method of transport was by air, as the Lido Road was impassable. For us this particular so-called invasion began one hot afternoon in late October. The heat was intense, and everyone was feeling rather limp. New admissions usually arrived during the afternoon. This particular day Sister was off duty and Scottie and I were on our own and on Surgical Ward the stretcher bearers returned again and again along the covered alley from the Out-Patients Department with more and more patients. As fast as I could fill in their names on to a chart and direct them towards a bed, another stretcher was waiting with another patient, sometimes so badly wounded that it took time for Scottie and me assisted by the Indian Sepoys to lift the blanket he was lying on and lower him onto the bed. Soon there was a long queue waiting in the outer room. There was no time to undress the patient and he had to be left lying in his blood soaked jungle greens to be attended to later. Before long all the vacant beds inside the ward were full, then all the verandah beds were filled, then there were no more beds and still they came – so now they had to be left lying on their stretchers, all down the centre of the ward between the beds. Two Medical Officers, who were on duty that afternoon, an Indian and an RAMC Captain, had arrived and were dressing wounds. We never stopped for hours for when the casualties ceased arriving, we had to begin removing blood-soaked clothing, wash mud-caked faces, clean wounds, take temperatures, improvise pillows for those lying on the floor etc. etc. Luckily the weather was too hot for blankets for bedding had long since run out.

This was the scene which met Sister's eyes when she called back from her half day off, she had gone off to the local Bazaar to do some shopping. She walked onto her ward, but there was no longer confusion, we had got everything more or less under control and patients were being made as comfortable as possible. For some days after this there was no off-duty for any of us and it was also necessary to stay on long after the night staff came on duty in order to get the work done. This is a personal incident which I mention taking place in one ward in one frontline hospital, but just the same thing was going on at other times in other hospitals where Red Cross and St John's Ambulance VADs were working, depending on in which area of the front the fighting had flared up, angels of mercy doing their best to alleviate pain and suffering and sometimes just give a little feminine company and share a joke.

By Christmas there was very little military activity in northern Assam where we were, as the majority of the fighting had moved south and the Japanese were being pushed back towards Rangoon, so we were not so busy in the hospital as we had been, especially in the surgical Ward where I was, for this was where the battle casualties were brought although the medical and malaria wards were still busy. We were able to enjoy ourselves and we certainly did. We did our best to decorate the wards and Winchester enlisted the help of the walking patients to give the place a festive air so there was little for us to do. On Christmas Eve the Sisters and Nurses gave a party for the other ranks and Orderlies in our Mess, which of course included Scottie and Winchester and was a great success. Christmas Day was really very much like any other day, I tried to cheer my patients up,

Myself outside the nurses quaters

they were obviously feeling sad and lonely and thinking of home and their loved ones. This situation of course did not arise on most of the other wards which were mainly Indian.

There were a lot of troops stationed in the area around the hospital, both British and Americans, and very soon after our arrival the word spread around that a batch of young nurses had just arrived at 49

Indian British General Hospital and they descended on us in droves. The officers used to motor over from their camps in jeeps, trucks, lorries or any transport they could lay their hands on. There was nowhere much to go, but a drive to the nearest native village and a walk through the bazaar was always fun and sometimes it included a meal at one of the local eating places. We still kept very much to our twosomes rather than going out in a group. Marion Parsonage and I went out regularly with a couple of Americans, one was Earl Cullum. Sometimes the officers and also the other ranks would give a little party in their various camps and we would all be asked. One thought nothing of motoring 30 or 40 miles over appalling tracks to one of these parties. There would be dancing to a gramophone, and as you can imagine, with so few white women in the area, we were very much in demand and we all felt we had become Beauty Queens overnight!

Earlier on, when the intense fighting was at its height at Imphal and the Lido Road this was not the case, but by the time we arrived most of this activity had died down, with the exception of the fighting which had flared up at Pen-Wei when we were all so busy there was no question of going out to parties.

It was just before Christmas that I met Graham Atcherly-Wright. He was serving with the RIAS Corps, and they gave a party in their Mess to which we were invited. They had arranged a Paul Jones, which is a dance where the men go round in a circle one way and the girls the other way and when the music stops you dance with the person opposite you. In this case of course there were far more men than girls, we were in the middle, and whenever the music stopped there was always a lot of them left out. I remember so well this good looking Subaltern with dark hair and a moustache who always managed somehow to come to a halt opposite me, his eyes held mine, and for the rest of the evening we remained together. Next day he drove over to see me at the hospital and that was the beginning of a great romance. Graham would come over regularly to see me when I had come off duty, sometimes he would take me to the cinema at the Officers Club, other times we would go in his jeep to the bazaar, or we would have dinner in the Officers Mess. One night he came over bringing a duck and green peas with all the trimmings and a bottle of wine and we had a very fine picnic dinner in my room. Fortunately Marion was on night duty at that time! Just after New Year he took me to Dibrugarh, which was about a 40 mile drive and we stayed the night at a tea planters bungalow with a friend of his called Eric Keyes. It was so lovely to be in a private house with all the comforts we had been denied for so long. It was a marvellous evening, waited on by bearers and served iced drinks on the terrace. The tea planters on the whole lived in great luxury and Eric was an excellent host. Alas! we had to leave very early next morning as I had to be on duty on the ward at 8 o'clock. For some weeks we had an idyllic time together, Graham would come onto the ward making friends with the patients and bringing them little luxuries from his mess and one evening he took Winchester out for a meal. At this time Marion was on leave spending some time with her husband, an RAMC Major who was serving with a hospital in India, so I was on my own in my room and when I came off duty Graham would always be there. Sometimes we would invite Captain Smith the Surgeon and Major Higgs the Medical Officer and others, Graham would bring whisky from his Mess and we would have a little party. They were happy days.

One Sunday I had the day off, we went on the river and had curry for lunch and on the way back Graham told me he was married and had a small son at home. I was absolutely shattered, it was such a shock. He hastened to reassure me, saying that the marriage had not been going well and he would get a divorce after he got back to England and then we could get married, but I had heard of too many of my friends back home who got involved with married men and had waited for the promised divorce, which never came and I knew that after the war, when we were all back in England things would be so different and that might well be the case with him. I still remember today how I felt as we drove along after he had broken this awful news to me.

The following week he arrived at the hospital in an awful state of depression and said that he would be leaving in a few days as orders had come through for his posting to another unit. We tried to make the most of those few days together and I knew that in spite of everything I would miss him terribly. The few days passed very quickly. Everyone on the ward was sorry including Sister Francis who had taken a liking to him. After he left I felt very flat and depressed. I missed him terribly. We had had a lot of fun together and I had grown very fond of him but I immersed myself into my work and went to bed early, catching up on some much needed sleep.

It is said that when one door closes another opens, and this was the case with me. I was coming off duty one day and I saw a tall familiar figure striding across the Compound towards me. It was Alastair, the Chindit Officer whom I had known in Poona. We had corresponded initially but I had not heard from him for a long while, the reason being he was heavily involved in Operation 'Capital', which included the West African Division which he was part of, steadily pressing forward with heavy fighting down the Kaladan Valley in the Arakan. They had at last linked up with units of the Fourteenth Army.

On 27 January Mountbatten, as Supreme Commander SEAC, signalled to Churchill and Roosevelt: 'the first part of the orders I received at Quebec has been carried out. The land route to China is open.' The West African Frontier Force were relieved of their duties and given leave. Most of them headed for Calcutta but Alastair hitched a lift on a plane heading for Dinjan, the local airfield for

Panitola. On arrival he went and stayed with some tea-planter friends of his called Morrisse and the next morning he made his way to the hospital. It was a lovely surprise, and we went to my room and sat and talked. He invited me over to dinner that evening at the Morisses and said he would come back after I came off duty and pick me up. The Morrises' plantation was lovely and the bungalow very luxurious. It was a lovely evening, Mrs Morrisse was charming and said that Alastair had talked a lot about me. The cook boy produced an excellent meal and afterwards we sat on the terrace watching the myriad of glowing fireflies and sipping cool drinks. The following afternoon he turned up at my room and said that he had been given a week's leave and he had come up to ask me to marry him. It was such a shock I did not known what to say. We had only known each other for about a week down in Poona, but during that time we had talked about our respective families, and I knew that he lived in Scotland, that his father was dead and he lived with his mother and younger sister at a lovely house with a lake called Meadowhead and that his elder brother John had inherited the Mackenzie Estate which consisted of many acres and tenant farms. Our backgrounds were similar and it would be a good marriage for me, one that my parents would approve of. But, I was not in love with him, I was still in love with Graham. What a quandary! The man I loved I couldn't have because he was married to somebody else. There was no question of let's wait and see, Alastair wanted to marry me now. He wanted to fly down to Calcutta with me the very next day. If I refused he would go away and I would probably never see him again. There was a war on then, people didn't make plans, such as long engagements. They got leave and they got married whilst they could, for no one knew what the future would bring. If Alastair left now, he would return to his unit and they might be posted anywhere. I had visions of the war ending and me returning to my home in Devon after my great adventure and Alastair returning to Scotland to be fêted by all the girls in Edinburgh and my parents' surprise that I should come home from India without finding anyone out there to marry. So I accepted his proposal and we went to find matron to obtain her permission. We had to pretend that we had known each other before in England otherwise she would never have agreed and she gave me leave to go to Calcutta the next day to get married. This caused for celebrations, so we went into the bazaar to have a few drinks and make our plans. Alastair would call for me the following morning and we would fly down to Calcutta in a troop plane. These had bucket seats around the walls to contain as many people as possible.

That evening, as I lay in my charpoi trying to get some sleep I heard a knock on the door. It was Graham. He had driven for hours from his new camp to be with me for a while as he said he had a presentiment that something was wrong. When I told him what had happened there was a terrible scene. He argued and cajoled and wept and did everything he could to talk me out of it but I wouldn't budge. I had made my decision and that was it. I finally got him to leave during the small hours of the morning. It was very distressing for me because I still loved him.

It seemed no time at all before Alastair arrived to take me to the airfield. I had never flown before, and was feeling more than some-what nervous. The plane was packed and more troops were waiting to come on. A seat was found for me along the wall but many people had to stand. It was not until afterwards that Alastair told me that we had only just cleared the runway on take off owing to the plane being very much overweight. On arrival I checked into the Young Womens Christian Association, and Alastair would be staying at the Grand. Then we went to the Cathedral to see the Dean. It's a small world, for of all the extraordinary coincidences he knew my father. When he heard my name he asked me if I was any relation to Jack Sloggett, a famous cricketer, whom he used to play with many years ago. When I told him that I was his daughter, he was delighted and asked warmly after my father and reminisced about the many exciting cricket matches that they had played together in the old days before he left his parish to serve his Church in India. After that there was no problem and he said that he would arrange for someone to marry us in the Cathedral within two days.

The next day we went to the best jeweller's shop in Calcutta to buy the rings, an engagement ring and a wedding ring. Alastair chose a square-cut emerald supported by two small diamonds each side, mounted on a platinum band. It was very beautiful. He had plenty of money, having been in the jungle for so many months and not able to spend his pay. The wedding ring, instead of being a plain gold band was platinum, studded with tiny diamonds.

Alastair had no problem finding a best man as many of his fellow officers were staying at the Grand, but I had a problem, who was I going to get to give me away in place of my father? The only person I knew in Calcutta was Bob Adams, the RAF Flight Lieutenant. I had flirted with on the ship coming out to India. He had given me his telephone number as he had a Staff job there, saying if ever I was in Calcutta on leave to be sure and ring him up. He was delighted to her from me again but his enthusiasm waned somewhat when I explained the purpose of my call, that I was getting married the next day and would he please give me away. However he agreed to do so, and we arranged that he should pick me up at the YWCA at 1.30 in time to be at the Cathedral by 2 o'clock. The problem of what to wear was simple as I only had one nice dress to wear which I had packed before leaving home, the pretty grey outfit with small buttons down the front, which I had last worn at the Turf Club in Poona, the night we were put into the corridor to eat and not accepted into the restaurant as I was not wearing a long dress! I went out shopping for a little hat and sewed a few silk flowers onto it. Today more than 50 years later I still have that photograph on the mantlepiece with Alastair in uniform, tropical bush jacket with the Chindit insignia and wearing his Royal Scots Glengarry. So different from other people's wedding photos!

Bob arrived as arranged looking very smart in RAF Mess Kit and we set off for the Cathedral. When we got there, everything looked very dead, not a soul to be seen, no sign of Alastair, what could have happened? Eventually we found an Indian dusting the stalls. 'Other Cathedral, Master,' he said to Bob. 'You mean there are two Cathedrals here in Calcutta?' 'Yes, Master,' he replied and went on with his work. 'Where is the other Cathedral?' I asked beginning to panic as it was now 2 p.m., but he merely shrugged his shoulders.

We eventually found our way to the new Cathedral and just in time, as no wedding could take place after 3 o'clock in the afternoon. We found Alastair and his best man waiting at the door, looking very worried as time was getting short. There were quite a few people apart from some Army Officers who had been invited, casual people passing by and some photographers. Alastair handed me a beautiful bouquet of flowers and went inside to wait for Bob and me. The organ played 'Here comes the Bride' and the Bishop performed a very nice service. Afterwards we all retired to the Grand Hotel where Alastair had organised a Wedding Reception which everyone enjoyed.

That evening with all the guests gone we danced to the hotel orchestra. Next day we went to the races. The Indians are mad about horse racing and love to gamble. It was a very colourful sight with all the ladies in their beautiful saris and bands playing.

The next few days passed only too quickly. I had been given a week's leave and the first three days had been spent arranging the wedding, so far too soon it was time for me to go back and for Alastair to rejoin his unit who were now stationed in Madras. I felt very depressed flying back from Calcutta to Dinjan. I had become very fond of Alastair and we had been very happy together during those few days.

Within a few days of my return, I was told that I was to go on night duty. I suppose this was fair as most of others had done their turn and I had not. What a way to be greeted, I though after my lovely, albeit brief, honeymoon, for the night was alive with noises and unknown hazards and now I was to be put on night duty.

Chapter Five

NIGHT DUTY WAS ARDUOUS and full of unknown hazards. The term of night duty was a fortnight, not a month as it was in England. This was to avoid too much strain on the nurses, for sleeping during the great heat of the day was sometimes very difficult, and the night duty itself was arduous for there was only one Sister and one VAD with a few orderlies for the whole of the hospital. Sister had so many wards under her care and the VAD had the remainder. One did not wear a dress and cap at night, but jungle green bush jacket with trousers, sleeves rolled down on account of malaria precautions and to protect one's arms and legs. As I explained earlier something of the layout of the hospital, the reader will realise this meant walking outside in the open from one ward to another, carrying a butti (which was the local name for a hurricane lamp). The night was alive with noises, glow-worms, flying ants etc. The jackals used to come right into the hospital compound sometimes, and their eerie barking made a most frightening sound. The isolation ward was somewhat apart and to go down there on one's 2 hourly round was always something of an ordeal for those inclined to be nervous. The end doors of the wards were always left open at night to give some air, and one night I walked into a ward during a routine round and found a new patient on the end bed, which before had been empty – it was a goat who had wandered in and found himself a comfortable place to spend the night!

It was on my second night on duty when I was told to special a patient on the officers ward. He was so ill it was considered necessary for him to have a nurse sitting with him all night. I had a very harrowing time for the man was quite delirious and fought me with surprising strength several times during the night to get out of bed, having torn the Ryles tube out which was draining the poison out of his side, also the needle administering the blood transfusion, placed there earlier by the Medical Officer. His name was Major Marshall and after he had torn his tubes out I sent an orderly to fetch the Duty MO for I was having such trouble restraining him. The latter gave him an injection to calm him down and shortly after he died. It was about 3 a.m., that hour of the night when those on night duty feel at their lowest. It was the first time I had seen a dead person. I called Sister and after she had certified him dead, she turned to me and said, 'Lay him out Nurse and make him look nice.' At first I thought I must have heard her wrong, it wasn't possible that she was going to leave me to do this by myself, but by now she had walked away and I had not heard her wrong. For a while I stared in horror, I did not feel I could touch him, especially after all the trouble I had had with him earlier, and how he had fought me with surprising strength in his delirium, and now to go and die on me like this, what a rotten thing to do. I felt no sympathy for him, only a feeling of revulsion. By now rigor mortis was setting in, so I ran across the grass to the nearby ward, a thing we were told never to do for fear of leeches, snakes and scorpions, but to approach the neighbouring ward along the concrete pathways adjoining them. I found the night orderly on duty. He was a kind little Cockney and seeing the state I was in felt sorry for me, took my arm in a fatherly manner and escorted me back to my ward, whereupon he did the job for me with a running commentary, in case, he said, another occasion might arise and then I would know what to do. The RMC Orderlies were highly trained and knew their jobs from long experience, unlike me, a trembling 20 year old who had never seen a dead body before.

A few nights later we heard that an American Negro killer had got loose, having been held in custody at the US Camp near by. We were afraid that he might wander into the hospital after dark to seek shelter. Sister and I were very scared, and we did our rounds together that night. Next morning an American Officer who was a friend of mine called round to see me and told me that the man had been caught, which was a great relief. He had apparently been on the loose for several days.

Conversely, night duty could be quite pleasant, one could have a cup of tea stretch out and relax between doing the rounds and have a bit of shut eye. I was fortunate because an RAMC major whom I had a bit of a crush on had gone down with malaria and was in a private room on the Officers Ward, so I made regular visits to see him and sat chatting with him, which he seemed to enjoy as much as I did!

Finally the two weeks were over and my night duty finished and

The negro assassin captured near the hospital

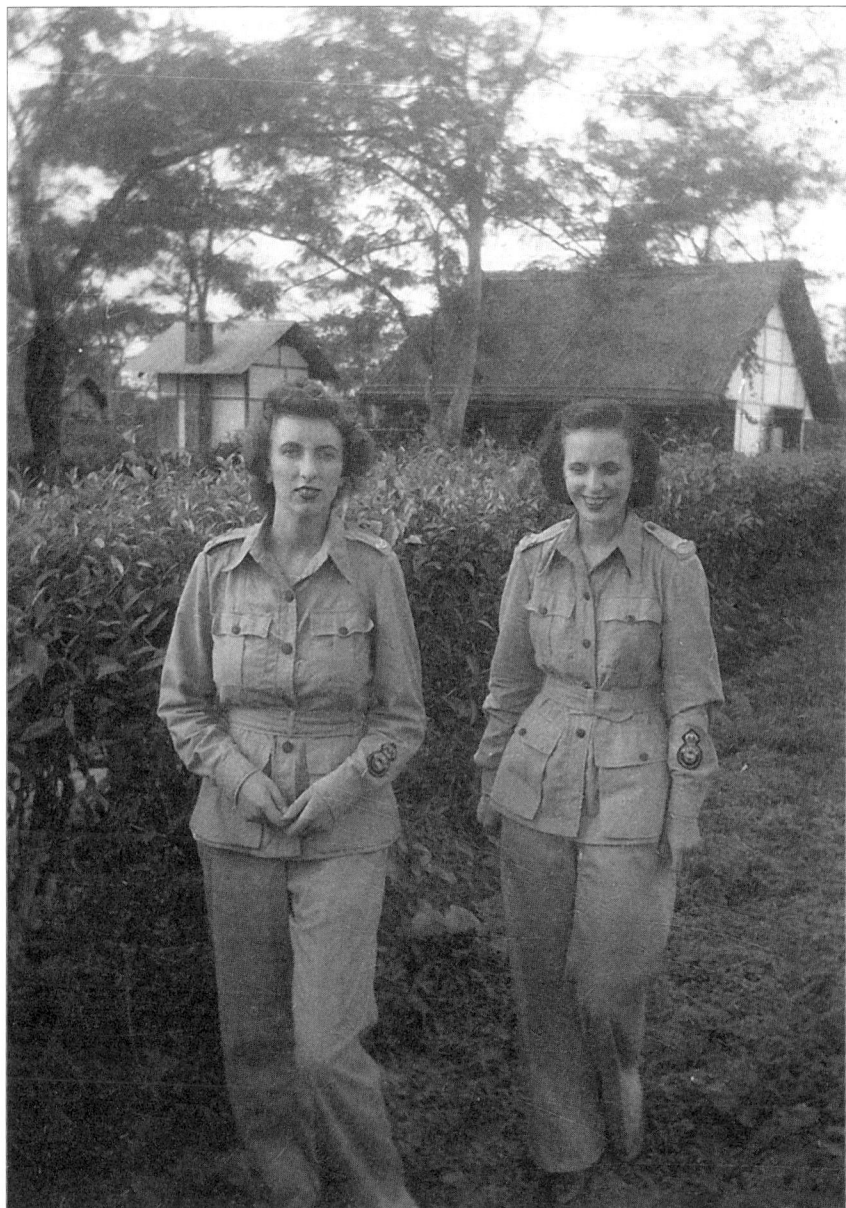

Marion Parsonage and myself in 'Jungle Greens'

I was told I was going to be transferred on to another ward. I was sorry about this for it meant leaving Scottie, the Cockney Orderly who had taught me so much, also Winchester, the walking patient, who was such a help and such a friend, and of course, it meant leaving Sister Francis whom I had served with right from the start.

Matron called me to her office. 'Ah, Nurse Sloggett,' she said. 'I am going to put you on the Dysentery Ward to look after alone, do you think you can do it? We are very short-staffed as Nurse Parsonage is going on leave.' This was in fact my best friend Marion, whose husband, a major in the RAMC, had asked permission for her to come and visit him for a while. I would miss her terribly, as we had been almost inseparable since leaving London, but she had been very highly trained before coming out and had served in London hospitals during the blitz, unlike me who had been mainly serving meals and bedmaking in my Convalescent Home near Salisbury. Even so, she wasn't the only one who had been on a ward alone, several of the older and more experienced ones had been in sole charge of a ward with perhaps two orderlies to help and as many as 40 patients or so under their care. Marion Robertson was in charge of the Isolation Ward by herself where patients were recovering from typhus. She did the rounds with the doctor, gave the treatments, wrote the daily report book and everything by herself, assisted by two RAMC Orderlies.

So I took over the Dysentery Ward. I would miss the others, but this was a step forward and I felt honoured that Matron had entrusted me with the responsibility of being in sole charge of a ward. By this time I had learnt quite a bit about the treatment of dysentery as it is very rife in the jungle. This disease is, as I have just mentioned, widespread in the tropics and inflicted many casualties amongst the troops – the amoeba which causes it can remain alive in water or damp soil for a considerable period, so you can see how easy it was for infection to spread from contaminated water, or food, or flies conveying the amoebic cysts from the latrines. The main treatment they used for this pernicious disease was regular emetine injections, but the percentage of those permanently cured by one course of treatment was not high, and very often patients had relapses on returning to the jungle and had to be sent back again.

To be on a ward by oneself meant less time off. In my absence two orderlies would be on duty overlooked by a Sister or VAD from a neighbouring ward who would come across to give the treatments or injections and write up the report, but this thrust a lot of extra work onto someone else who was already very busy on her own ward, so during very busy periods I hardly went off duty at all. This only applied to periods when there was a lot of activity taking place, otherwise if one was alone on a ward one normally took the off-duty period from 1 p.m. to 5 p.m. during which time patients were mostly resting. Out there it was very hot at that time and the only treatment done during the afternoon were TPRs (temperature, pulse, respiration) and bed-baths which a couple of orderlies were quite capable of doing. Then the nurse would return again from 5 p.m. to 8 p.m. to do dressings, give injections and write up the daily Report Book ready for the night staff. During busy periods I often remained on duty as late as 10 o'clock at night, long after the night shift had come on duty because I had not nearly finished my work, I found writing up the reports particularly onerous.

A few weeks after I had taken over the Dysentery Ward we were told that the hospital was moving as the casualties were now being flown out to Southern Assam. The authorities had decided that it would be better if we were at Dibrugarh, which was about 30 miles south, and so replace 45 IBGH which would in turn go forward towards Rangoon which was being held by the Japanese. We were all very sad to leave our happy little hospital at Panitola. There were very few patients left now and the Officers Ward was empty so the packing up began. It was a very big job to move all the beds, most of them were dismantled and put onto trucks and the smaller stuff was loaded into ambulances. In the Sisters' Mess everyone felt very depressed, all the remaining patients had been moved now and the place was empty and gloomy. The last thing to do was pack up our own sleeping quarters and the Sisters' Mess and leave the little hospital that we had been so proud of. All in all the packing up had taken several weeks.

When we arrived at Dibrugarh we found all in turmoil, some new wards were being built, it was desperately hot and everyone was shouting at once. Every bit of our equipment had to be changed over with that of the other hospital and at the same time we had to take over their patients. We still had our own matron in charge of us and the same sisters, but three of our VADs had left. My friend Marion Parsonage had left some while back, also two others to get married and be with their husbands. Although I also had got married I had come out from England to join Bill Slim's Fourteenth Army and nurse the wounded and I certainly wasn't going off as an Army wife to be with one's husband wherever he had been posted. The VADs of 45 IBGH had all been posted to other hospitals and so we were able to move into their rooms. Soon after the move to the hospital at Dibrugarh an official notice arrived asking everyone if they wished to be posted forward, and that meant Rangoon. All the VADs promptly signed, 'Yes', but the QAs who had been out there much longer than us, and had been the reason why Lady Louis Mountbatten had sent us out to relieve the over worked QAs in the first place, said, 'No'.

They had had enough and sadly most of our sisters were posted back to India and new ones arrived in their places.

It was whilst we were at Dibrugarh that I was put on the Indian VD Ward which I referred to earlier, saying how shocked my father had been. It was the first time I had worked on an Indian Ward having been always on British Wards and I knew very little about their superstitions and religious dogma. In their eyes we were considered unclean and so could never touch their food or drink. Instead of the RAMC Orderlies they had nursing sepoys and their duties again were decreed by caste, and I made myself very unpopular on my first day by instructing a sepoy to give a patient a bedpan. I did not know, but this was one thing they simply would not do. This was the sweeper's job who washed the floors and looked after the latrines. I had one RAMC Orderly to help me. His name was Ernie and I don't what I would have done without him, for he knew all about the caste system and had been working on the ward when there was a Sister in charge. I never knew how they managed in the fighting lines about these rules as I couldn't speak the language. I asked one of the other VADs who had been on an Indian Ward and she did not seem to know either.

Pte. Tyne. T.
9th Royal Sussex
45 I.G.H.
12.12.44

Dear Miss Sloggett

Trusting that you do not think I'm taking any liberties in writing to you. I must thank you once again for what you did for the boys, because they greatly appreciated what you did for them. It is grand to know that we have people like yourself to look after us, because if it was left to the other people I don't know where we would finish up at times. Hoping that you are getting along quite well. I suppose you still have plenty to do and plenty of dashing around. [part missing] you would be sorry to [illegible] him because you get plenty of fun out of him. Remember me to sister Francis. I'm going along alright now, I expect to be going out shortly. I'll close with A Merry Xmas and A Happy New Year to all.

A friend T. Tyne.

My sources of information for this book come from letters written home to parents and family which had been kept, from notes written immediately I got back to England, the lecture I gave to the Wiltshire Division of the SJAB on my return, some of it from memory and most important from my diary, which I meticulously kept and has enabled me to put things in chronological order. Looking inside my diary I see that I had arranged a complicated code for letters home, as all our mail was censored. To quote a few Dimapur = Egbert, Kohima = Charles, somewhere near Japanese = George, South = Arthur, am moving = Geoffrey and so on.

I see that I have written in my diary, 'hate it on this ward, am very depressed.' During that time Germany surrendered and at home the VE day celebrations were taking place, but as far as we were concerned there was little rejoicing. Our war was still going on, we were still fighting the Japs and the boys of the 14th Army were still in the thick of it. Luckily we did not stay long at Dibrugarh as news came through that the promised move to Rangoon was to take place. So luckily for me my stint on VD Ward was short lived.

The arrangements were that the nursing staff were to go to a transit camp at Chittagong and from there we should go on a Troopship to Rangoon to join our hospital 49 IBGH.

On arrival at Chittagong, we were billeted in a block with some QAs who were waiting to go on to Rangoon too. It was an extraordinary building consisting of three floors with rooms rather like cages, open at one end giving onto a balcony. We did not have to share, but were each given a room to ourselves. We were told that whilst we were there, we would be employed at the Field Hospital up the hill. The other way, down the hill, led to a lovely beach, where we bathed and the water was warm and glorious. I made friends with a young and very good looking officer and he took me for rides in his jeep when I wasn't working, and to parties in his mess. One day when I was off duty and sitting on my balcony I saw a familiar figure striding across the compound towards me. It was Alastair. It appeared that he had been released from his unit to go to the Staff College at Quetta. I had written him that we were in transit at Chittagong en route to Rangoon. He told me that he would have a lovely bungalow with a garden and servants and could have his wife with him. In short, he had come to fetch me. I was appalled. Instead of going on to Rangoon with the other VADs and all the excitement I was to be expelled to some luxury bungalow in India leaving all my comrades to go on without me. What was I to do? 'I don't think Matron will let me go,' I said hopefully. 'The VADs will be needed to deal with the casualties.'

'Well, let's go and see Matron,' he said. Miss Sherborne was the same matron who had been with us at Panitola, and had given us permission to go off and get married. So we went to see Matron. I looked at her in agony, trying to make her read my thoughts and understand that I did not want to go with my husband and hoping she would say that she could not spare me. But, when Alastair explained the situation, she said, 'Of course Major Mackenzie, I quite understand, it is quite natural that you should want to have your wife with you out in Quetta. You have hardly seen each other since you got married, and with your brave exploits with the Chindits you deserve it. Good luck.' So I never got to Rangoon.

Chapter Six

Quetta

THE JOURNEY TOOK MANY DAYS, first of all a long slow train journey to Calcutta, where we stayed the night and then on by another train and finally a bus up through the hills. I was feeling very flat and depressed, having left all my comrades to go on without me, but I tried not to show it as Alastair was so full of enthusiasm.

On arrival we were met by the bearer from the bungalow which had been allocated to us. It was indeed a lovely house, large and roomy with a big garden in the corner of which was a solid concrete building which was a shelter against earthquakes.

It was terribly hot and we slept out of doors still needing nothing but a sheet. There were several servants and an amah to look after me. We soon made friends with the other officers and their wives in the surrounding bungalows and were invited out to drinks and dinner parties which was all great fun, and we used to go and swim at the Officers Club, where we often had wild parties of an evening with a lot of drink being consumed. After a while I got bored with this life and decided to go and see the Matron of the Indian British General Hospital there, and asked if I could do some voluntary work. It was arranged that I go from 9 a.m. to 1 p.m. daily. I was put on the Indian Surgical Ward to help with all the dressings. I used to cycle down and return on a tonga with my bike loaded on, as it was uphill all the way.

This life continued for some while until one August morning Alastair returned home just when I had got back from work with the news that some awful bomb had been dropped by the Americans on a place in Japan called Hiroshima, that it had devastated the whole city in one go and thousands of people were killed. Apparently the damage was appalling and the flash as it exploded had electrocuted people on the spot. Two days later another of these awful bombs had been dropped on another town and the following day Japan conceded defeat and sued for peace. The war was over.

This gave rise to many celebrations and parties and our house was inundated at all hours of the day and night with friends rolling in armed with bottles, celebrating Victory Day.

Shortly after this I discovered that I was pregnant and Matron at the hospital decided that it was unwise for me to go on working there in case of infection for the unborn child. Also, as Alastair's course at the college was nearing its end, it was decided that I should go home. I was to be sent to a holding unit near Bombay and wait for a ship there to go back to England. It was a very long journey and I hated leaving all the friends that I had made in Quetta. I was very depressed and cried a lot in the train going down.

I remained in this holding unit for about a month, bored stiff, as there was nowhere much to go and nothing much to do. I did however have the company of some other nurses, VADs that I did not know and some QAs also waiting to go home.

On the 27 October at midday we sailed from Bombay. I have written in my diary, 'My feelings are mixed, I would not have missed this adventure for anything, now it is all over.' As we left the troops were surprisingly quiet.

Sunday 28 October. After all this time, on our first day at sea no one seems to be showing the enthusiasm one would have expected at their return home. There is still a feeling of negative flatness in the air which is hard to explain, the troops are still unaccountably quiet. Perhaps it is the terrible heat and the fact that the ship is so very overcrowded, or perhaps they are thinking of their many comrades in arms left behind in shallow little graves in Burma. 'When you go home, tell them of us, and say, for your tomorrow we gave our today.'

We had our first sight of England on 14th November and I have written in my diary. 'As I walk off the ship I start a different life, my adventures are over.' But I was 20 years old then, and now that I am an old lady I can truly say that my adventures were not over and that I have had a wonderful life and many exciting times since I was a VAD in Burma.

THE END

Epilogue

Farewell to the '14th'

GENERAL SLIM'S MESSAGE to the Famous Army which disbands today and passes into history.

When you were first formed I told you that you could become one of the best-known armies the British Empire ever had, and so you did. Inheriting a legacy of defeat and disaster, constantly short of equipment, men and nurses, you by your stubborn courage, your skill, and above all by your refusal to be beaten by man or nature, achieved a success few thought possible.

If in the years to come you meet an old comrade down on his luck, give him a hand. When things go wrong stick it out. Work and fight as you did in Kohima, at Imphal and through Burma. Remember you were of the 14th Army, and never say die.

I send each one of you my thanks, my admiration, and my confidence that in peace as in war, the men and women of the 14th will play a noble part.'

The '14th' grew out of the rearguard of Indian divisions known as the Burma Corps. It killed more Japanese soldiers than were accounted for by all the rest of the Allied Forces in the Pacific theatre in some of the worst conditions in the world. Over 100,000 dead were actually counted. Twenty VCs were won.

At the peak of its achievements – spring 1945 – The 14th Army included amongst other English Regiments, the Royal Scots Fusiliers, The Royal Scots, The Cameron Highlanders and a detachment of VAD Nurses.